Georgia

BY MARLEY RICHMOND

Kids Core
An Imprint of Abdo Publishing
abdobooks.com

abdobooks.com

Published by Abdo Publishing, a division of ABDO, PO Box 398166, Minneapolis, Minnesota 55439. Copyright © 2025 by Abdo Consulting Group, Inc. International copyrights reserved in all countries. No part of this book may be reproduced in any form without written permission from the publisher. Kids Core™ is a trademark and logo of Abdo Publishing.

Printed in China.
052024
092024

Cover Photo: Sean Pavone/Shutterstock Images
Interior Photos: Bettmann/Getty Images, 4–5, 7; Karel Bock/Shutterstock Images, 8 (top left); Serge Skiba/Shutterstock Images, 8 (top right); Shutterstock Images, 8 (bottom left), 20–21, 22, 28 (bottom); Lorraine Hudgins/Shutterstock Images, 8 (bottom right); Deborah Ferrin/Shutterstock Images, 10; Matt Hamilton/Chattanooga Times Free Press/AP Images, 12–13; Andrea Smith/AP Images, 15; John Adams/Icon Sportswire/Getty Images, 16, 28 (top right); Joseph Sohm/Shutterstock Images, 19; William Silver/Shutterstock Images, 25; iStockphoto, 26; Red Line Editorial, 28 (top left), 29

Editor: Laura Stickney
Series Designer: Katherine Hale

Library of Congress Control Number: 2023949342

Publisher's Cataloging-in-Publication Data

Names: Richmond, Marley, author.
Title: Georgia / by Marley Richmond
Description: Minneapolis, Minnesota: Abdo Publishing, 2025 | Series: Discovering the United States | Includes online resources and index.
Identifiers: ISBN 9781098293802 (lib. bdg.) | ISBN 9798384913078 (ebook)
Subjects: LCSH: U.S. states--Juvenile literature. | Georgia--History--Juvenile literature. | Southeastern States--Juvenile literature. | Physical geography--United States--Juvenile literature.
Classification: DDC 973--dc23

All population data taken from:
"Estimates of Population by Sex, Race, and Hispanic Origin: April 1, 2020 to July 1, 2022." *US Census Bureau, Population Division*, June 2023, census.gov.

CONTENTS

Members of the Albany Movement gather in the alley outside the city's jail.

The Albany Movement

It was December 15, 1961. A group of Black people gathered in Albany, Georgia. They were working together as part of the Albany Movement. Their goal was to end racial **segregation**. That night, Martin Luther King Jr. stood in front of them.

King was a leader in the civil rights movement. Across the United States, people were working to win equal rights for Black people. At that time, Black people in the South were forced to stay separated from white people. They couldn't go to the same schools or restaurants. In Albany, King spoke to the crowd. He celebrated their work. After his speech, the crowd sang about freedom. Their voices rose as one.

The next day, hundreds of Black people marched through the streets of Albany. Many were arrested, including King. At first, it looked as though the Albany Movement had failed. Black people would have to remain separated from white people.

Protesters flooded the streets of Albany, Georgia, to protest segregation in December 1961.

Things did not change right away. But months later, the city legally ended segregation. The civil rights movement continued to grow. Activists such as those in Albany made a huge difference in Georgia and other states.

Georgia Facts

DATE OF STATEHOOD
January 2, 1788

CAPITAL
Atlanta

POPULATION
10,912,876

AREA
59,425 square miles
(153,910 sq km)

STATE BIRD

Brown thrasher

STATE TREE

Live oak

STATE FLOWER

Cherokee rose

STATE AMPHIBIAN

Green tree frog

Each US state has a different population, size, and capital city. States also have state symbols.

Land and Climate

Georgia is in the region of the United States called the South. It is bordered by Florida to the south and Alabama to the west. Tennessee and North Carolina are to the north. South Carolina lies to the east. The southeastern part of the state borders the Atlantic Ocean.

The Appalachian Mountains are in northern Georgia. The state's tallest mountain is in the Appalachians. It is called Brasstown Bald. **Foothills** stretch across the middle of the state. This area is known as the Piedmont.

The Peach State

Georgia is known for growing delicious peaches. The hot, humid weather is perfect for this fruit. Peach orchards are found in the central and southern parts of the state. From mid-June to mid-July, Georgians can taste some of the sweetest peaches in the country.

Alligators are a common sight in the Okefenokee Swamp.

The Coastal Plain makes up the southern part of Georgia. This land is flat and has many **marshes**. The Okefenokee Swamp is in the lower Coastal Plain. It is a large wildlife **refuge**. Plants such as ferns, water lilies, and tall grasses grow there. Storks and herons wade through the water. Black bears, deer, otters, alligators, and green tree frogs can also be found in the swamp.

The climate in Georgia is generally warm. Summers are hot and humid. Rain falls often. In winter, the state cools down. But temperatures remain mild. Snow rarely falls outside of the mountains.

Explore Online

Visit the website below. Does it give any new information about the Okefenokee Swamp that wasn't in Chapter One?

Wildlife

abdocorelibrary.com/discovering-georgia

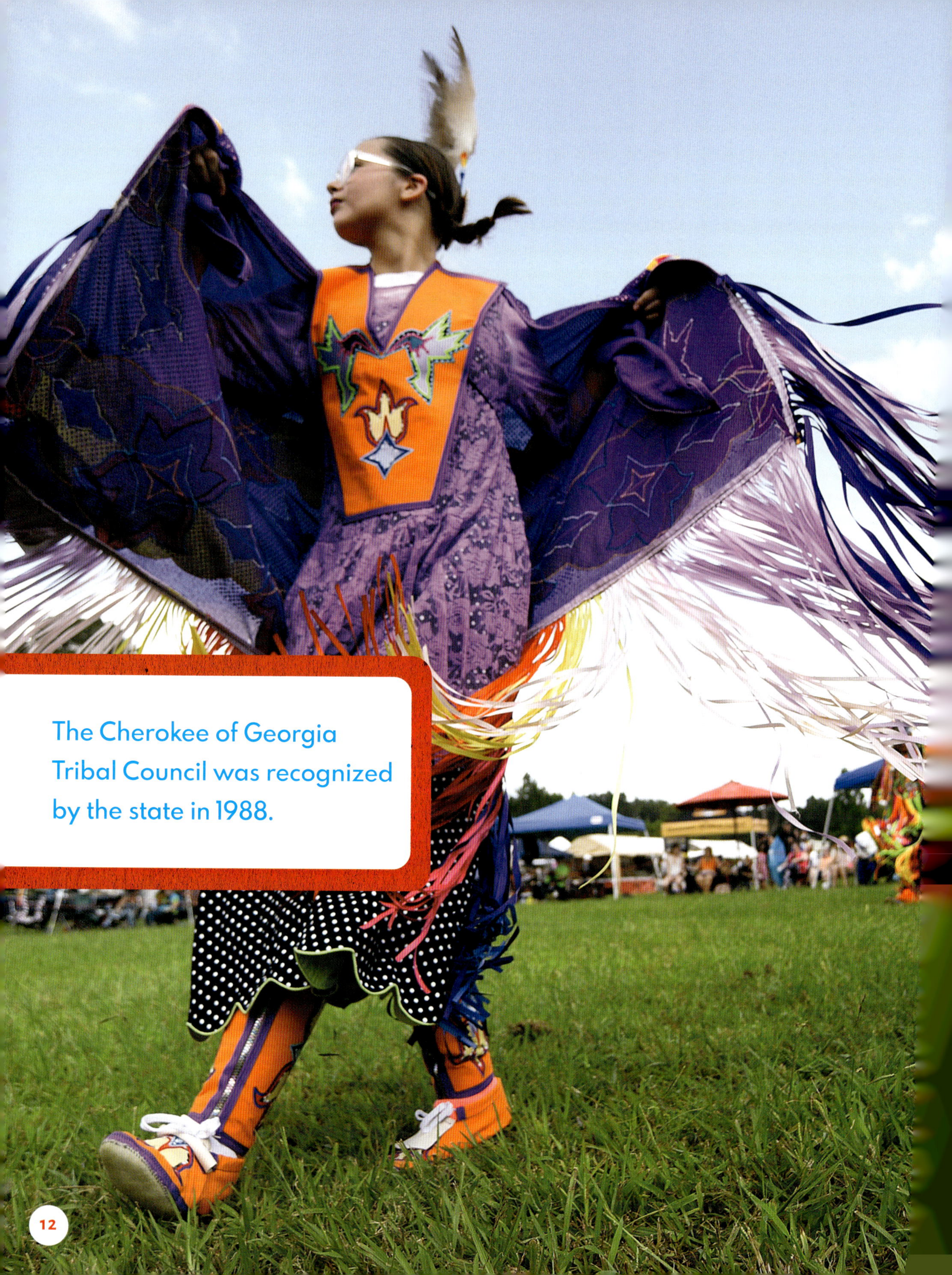

The Cherokee of Georgia Tribal Council was recognized by the state in 1988.

The People of Georgia

American Indian peoples have lived in what is now Georgia for more than 10,000 years. The Muscogee (or Creek) and Cherokee peoples were two major nations in the area. They were hunters and farmers.

Europeans arrived beginning in the 1600s. In the 1800s, many Cherokee and Muscogee people were forced to leave their homes. But these nations are still part of Georgia. They are now federally recognized tribes. They have their own governments and land.

Today, there are about 11 million people in Georgia. Less than 1 percent of Georgians are American Indian. About 5 percent are Asian. Another 10 percent are Hispanic or Latino. Black people make up 33 percent of the population. About 50 percent of Georgians are white.

Culture in Georgia

Food is an important part of Georgia's culture. Many popular dishes include ingredients that

Georgia farmers produce about 100 million bushels of peaches per year.

are farmed in the state. This includes peaches, peanuts, pecans, and Vidalia onions.

Soul food is common too. These recipes are connected to Black culture and history. Fried chicken, fried green tomatoes, and biscuits and gravy are popular types of soul food in Georgia.

Sports are also important to Georgia's culture. Many Georgians watch football.

An English bulldog named Uga has been the mascot of the University of Georgia since the 1950s. Uga XI became the school's mascot in 2023.

They might root for the University of Georgia Bulldogs or the Atlanta Falcons. NASCAR races also bring in big crowds. The Masters is a famous golf tournament. It is held in Augusta, Georgia, every year.

Many famous people were born in Georgia. Martin Luther King Jr. is from Atlanta. Jackie Robinson broke baseball's color barrier in 1947. He was born in Cairo, Georgia.

The Ring Shout

The ring shout is a spiritual dance from Central and West Africa. It was practiced by many enslaved people in the United States as far back as the 1840s. The dance helps connect people to their culture. Dancers move in a circle. They sing, clap, and tap their feet. Ring dances are still performed in Georgia.

Working in Georgia

Many Georgians work in the manufacturing industry. They make goods that will be sold. Clothing, fabric, paper, and **lumber** are just some of the products made in Georgia.

One major company in Georgia is Coca-Cola. The company's famous drink was invented by John Pemberton in Atlanta. It was first sold in 1886.

Further Evidence

Look at the website below. Does it give any new evidence to support Chapter Two?

Georgia

abdocorelibrary.com/discovering-georgia

The World of Coca-Cola is a popular tourist destination in Atlanta.

A moving walkway takes visitors underneath one of the tanks at the Georgia Aquarium in Atlanta.

Places in Georgia

There are many popular places to visit in Georgia. Atlanta is the state's capital. It is home to the Georgia Aquarium. This is the largest aquarium in North America.

The National Center for Civil and Human Rights is in Atlanta.

The National Center for Civil and Human Rights opened in 2014.

Visitors there can learn about Georgia's history. The museum shares stories of people who fought for equal rights. It also shows items such as books and papers that belonged to Martin Luther King Jr.

Columbus is another large city in Georgia. It is located in the western part of the state. Columbus has many museums. One is the National Civil War Naval Museum. There, visitors can tour **replicas** of ships that sailed during the American Civil War (1861–1865).

Spooky Savannah

Savannah, Georgia, is known as one of the most haunted places in the United States. It is home to the Marshall House. Visitors say this hotel is haunted. Some have seen ghosts in the halls. At Bonaventure Cemetery, people tell stories about the spirit of a girl named Gracie Watson. Visitors have reported seeing Gracie's ghost near her grave.

Parks

Georgia is home to Cumberland Island National Seashore. Cumberland Island is on the state's southern coast. It has marshes, beaches, and forests. Sea turtles, wild horses, and armadillos live there. People can take boats to the island. They can hike or camp.

Kolomoki Mounds State Park is near Blakely. People lived there thousands of years ago. They built mounds of earth and rocks. Some were probably **burial** mounds. Others may have been used for **rituals**. Park visitors can learn about the mounds and their history.

Georgia has many things to do and see. Visitors can learn about the state's long, rich history and the first peoples who lived there.

To help protect the land and wildlife, only 300 people are allowed on Cumberland Island each day.

The 13 stars on Georgia's flag are a symbol of the original 13 American colonies.

They can try popular soul foods and visit cities such as Atlanta and Columbus. The Peach State has something for everyone.

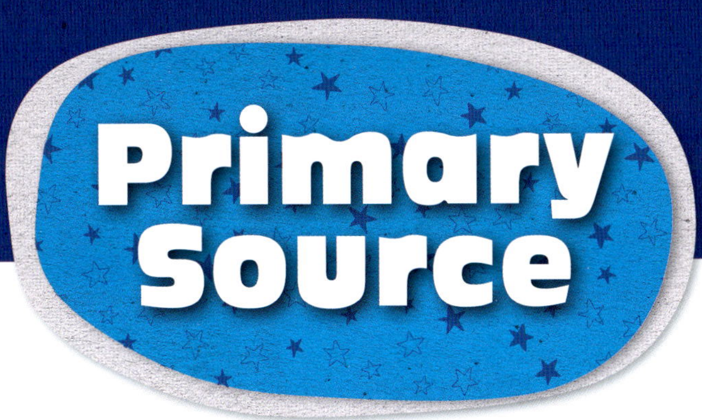

Scientists work at the Georgia Aquarium. The aquarium's website says:

> Our team conducts [important] research by working with animals both in human care and in their natural habitats. . . . Researchers in the Aquarium's exhibits and labs are learning more about [sea] life in order to develop new methods of animal care.

Source: "Research and Conservation Overview." *Georgia Aquarium*, n.d., georgiaaquarium.org. Accessed 14 Sept. 2023.

What's the Big Idea?

What is this quote's main idea? Explain how the main idea is supported by details.

State Map

KEY

Point of interest

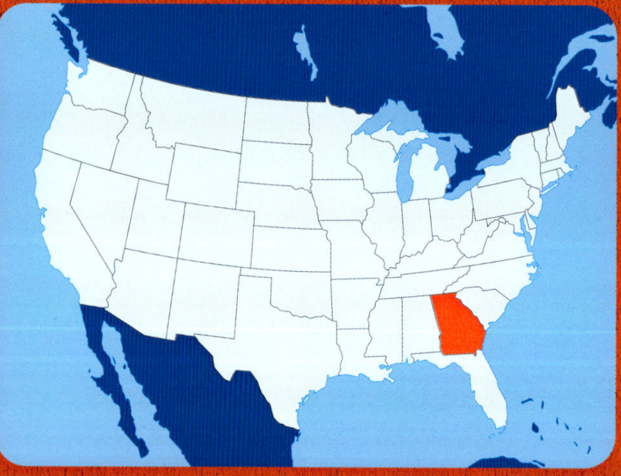

Uga XI

Georgia Aquarium

Georgia: The Peach State

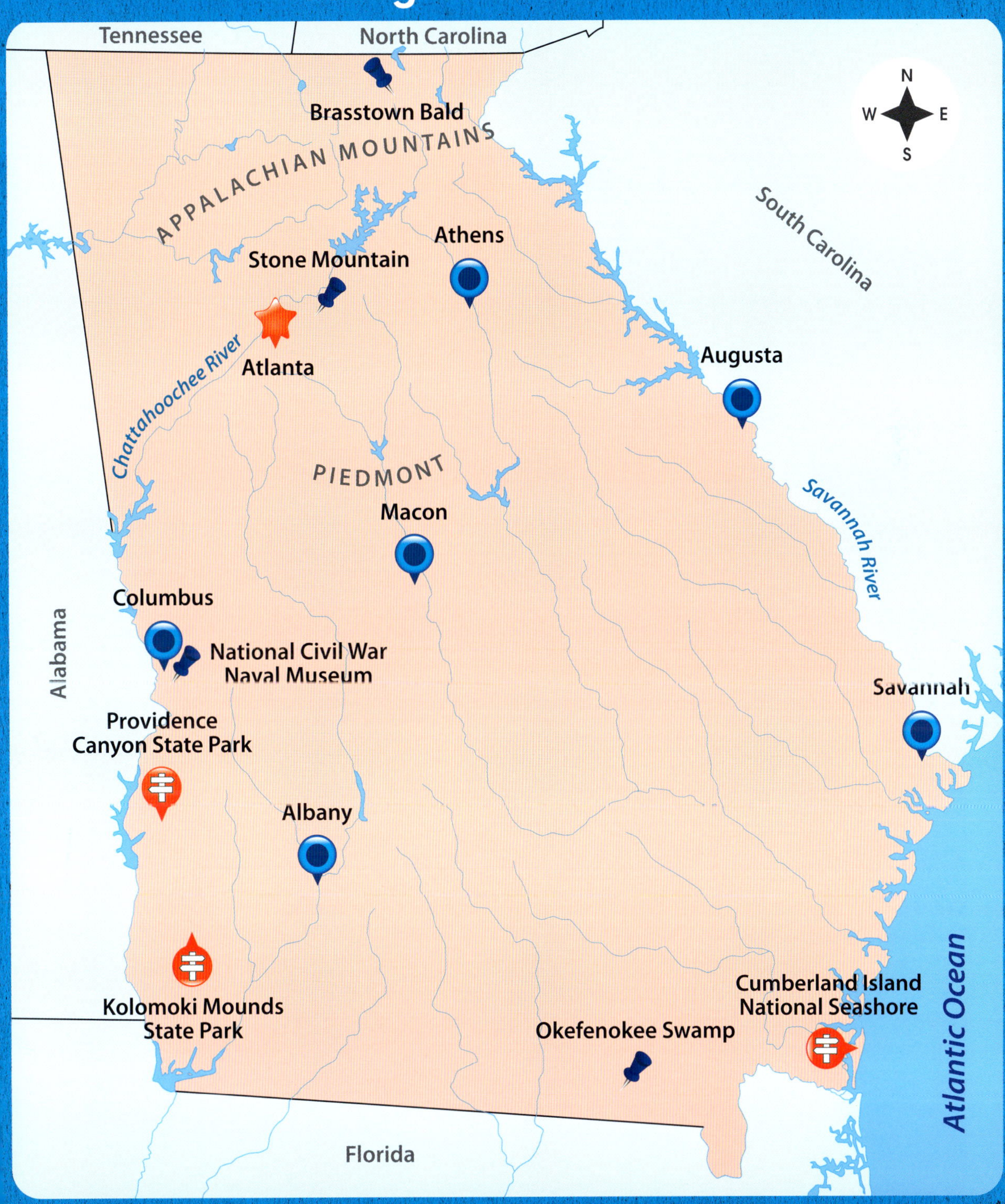

Glossary

burial
the act of placing a dead body in a grave

foothills
a hilly area at the base of a mountain range

lumber
logs used as building material

marshes
areas of soft wet land

refuge
a sheltered or protected place

replicas
exact copies of things

rituals
actions or traditions performed in a certain way

segregation
the separation of people by race or other characteristics

Online Resources

To learn more about Georgia, visit our free resource websites below.

Visit **abdocorelibrary.com** or scan this QR code for free Common Core resources for teachers and students, including vetted activities, multimedia, and booklinks, for deeper subject comprehension.

Visit **abdobooklinks.com** or scan this QR code for free additional online weblinks for further learning. These links are routinely monitored and updated to provide the most current information available.

Learn More

Hansen, Grace. *Martin Luther King Jr.: Civil Rights Activist.* Abdo, 2023.

Kavon, Kana. *The 50 States.* DK, 2021.

Tieck, Sarah. *Georgia.* Abdo, 2020.

Index

About the Author

Marley Richmond is a children's book editor and author. She lives in Minnesota with her cat, Bean.